NBA Game Day

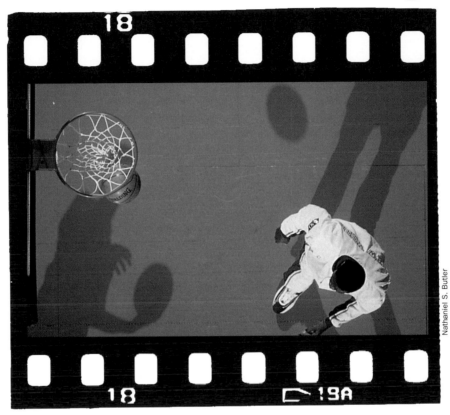

Fernando Medina

NBA Game Day

By Joe Layden and James Preller

SCHOLASTIC INC.

New York   Toronto   London   Auckland   Sydney

**Special thanks to
Eric Weinstein at NBA Entertainment—**
you are the man.

Library of Congress Cataloging-in-Publication Data
Layden, Joseph, 1959–
NBA Game Day by Joe Layden and James Preller   p.cm.
Summary: Photographs and text present an up-close look at varied aspects of the lives of professional basket-
ball players, from pre-game preparations, practice, game action, signing autographs, and more.
ISBN 0-590-76742-9
1. National Basketball Association—Pictorial works—Juvenile Literature. [1. Basketball. 2. National Basketball
Association.] I. Preller, James. II. Title
GV885.515.N37L37   1997
796.323.'64'0973—dc21   97–19257
CIP   AC

© 1997 by NBA Properties, Inc.
All rights reserved. Published by Scholastic Inc.

12 11 10 9 8 7 6 5 4 3 2 1   7 8 9/9 0 1 2/0

Printed in Mexico
First Scholastic printing, November 1997
Book design: Michael Malone

THE PHOTOGRAPHERS

PHOTOGRAPHER ANDREW D.
BERNSTEIN, SURROUNDED BY
THE TOOLS OF THE TRADE.

NBA Photo Library

Ray Amati • Bill Baptist • Gary Bassing
Andrew D. Bernstein • Nathaniel S. Butler
Louis Capozzola • Chris Covatta • Scott Cunningham
Gary Dineen • Garrett Ellwood • Sam Forencich
Ron Hoskins • David Liam Kyle • Mitchell Layton
Richard Lewis • Fernando Medina • Ronald C. Modra
Tim O'Dell • Christobal Perez • Jeff Reinking
Dave Sherman • Dale Tait • Sandy Tenuto
Noren Trotman • Ron Turenne • José Luis Villegas

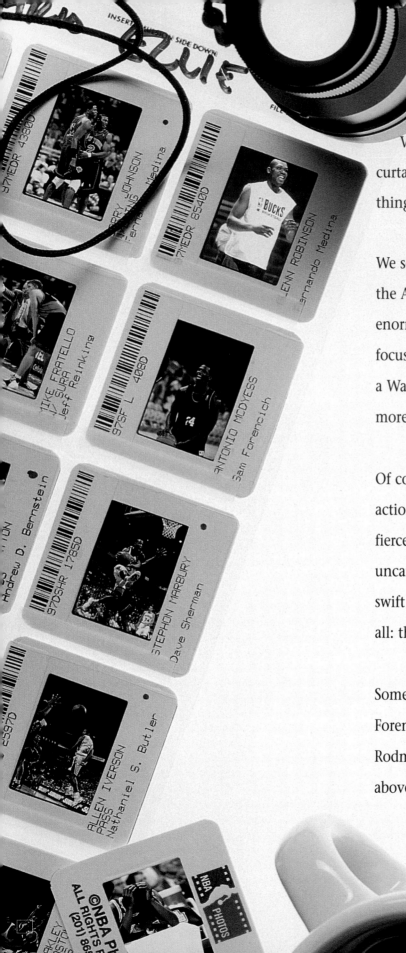

Viewing the photographs collected in this book is like having a curtain lifted for us, revealing a world we'd only guessed at. We see things not usually intended for our eyes.

We see, up close, Dikembe Mutombo chatting with Jon Barry on the Atlanta Hawks' team bus...Kevin Garnett sitting down to an enormous meal...Shaquille O'Neal, with wrapped ankle in sharp focus, leaning back on the trainer's table...Michael Jordan, wearing a Walkman, casually strolling in for a night's work...and so much more.

Of course, the heart of game day is the game itself: the end-to-end action, the fearless drives to the hole, the look-away passes and fierce rebounds. It is here where our photographers excel: their uncanny ability to capture lightning in a bottle. To take a game as swift as NBA basketball and, in one celluloid image, to convey it all: the energy, the drama, the breathtaking athleticism.

Sometimes one single image, such as Sam Forencich's near-miraculous photo of Dennis Rodman (pages 56-57)—seemingly afloat above the hardwood, fully horizontal, reaching out to corral a loose ball—conveys the essence of that player. Everything you need to know about Dennis Rodman, the basketball player, is in that one photograph.

In another favorite, captured by photographer Dave Sherman, we see the Minnesota Timberwolves in a huddle just moments before taking the floor. With hands clasped and fingers intertwined, it's as eloquent a team photo as you are likely to find.

To create this book, we called upon some of the finest sports photographers in the world—twenty-six are represented here—and gave them an open-ended, though daunting, task: *Show us what it is really like to play in the NBA.*

What follows, I believe, is not only a fascinating glimpse into life as it is actually lived in the NBA—it is proof positive that this talented group of photographers was up to the task. Enjoy the book.

—James Preller

Have you ever imagined

IT WASN'T TOO LONG AGO
WHEN THE NBA WAS ONLY A DREAM
FOR 21-YEAR-OLD **KEVIN GARNETT**.
NOW HE LIVES IT.

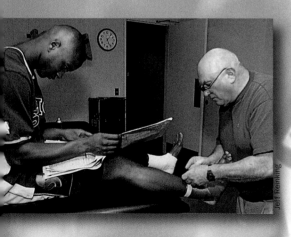

what it would be like to play in the NBA?

To glide down the court, matching strides with the greatest basketball players in the world? To hear the roar of the crowd as you throw down a dunk, or swat an opponent's shot into the bleachers?

It's every kid's dream.

And for the fortunate few who make it to the NBA, it's a dream come true.

Most NBA players know that they have just about the best job in the world. They're well paid. They travel on private jets. They stay in first-class hotels. They eat in the finest restaurants. Best of all, they get to play basketball—a game they love—every day.

It's a good life.

But it's not always an easy life. Basketball in the NBA is a job, and it's taken very seriously. Players work hard to reach the sport's highest level. And they have to *keep* working hard to stay there. The two hours in which they're on the court, performing for fans, playing the game, is only part of the picture. To get the complete story, you have to go behind the scenes: into the locker rooms and training rooms, on the bus, and at an early-morning practice.

A day in the life of an NBA player is a lot more hectic—and a lot longer—than you might imagine.

Just take a look....

The Atlanta Journal
THE ATLANTA CONSTITUTION

AMERICA'S NEWSPAPER
The Washington Times
Volume 4, No. 13   NATIONAL WEEKLY EDITION $2.50 (U.S.)

Houston Chronicle
Vol. 96   No. 161

VOLUME 251 ■ NUMBER 84
76 pages
50 cents
• • •
The Boston Globe
Today: Clouding, upper 40s
Tomorrow: Chance of showers, 60
High tide: 12:05 a.m., 12:05 p.m.
Full report: Page B9

The Charlotte Observer
www.charlotte.com

"All the News
That's Fit to Print"
The New York Times
VOL. CXLVI.... No. 50,742   Copyright © 1997 The New York Times
New York: Today, becoming cloudy, drizzle late. High 43. Tonight, rain, scattered fog. Low 43. Tomorrow, periods of rain. High 53. Yesterday, high 48, low 36. Details are on page C18.
$1 beyond the greater New York metropolitan area.   +   60 CENTS

Scott Cunningham

JON BARRY AND **DIKEMBE MUTOMBO** ON THE ATLANTA HAWKS' TEAM BUS.

Another day.

Another city.

The NBA season is one long road trip. Game day

begins in the early-morning hours, as the sun slices

through curtains in a quiet hotel room. A glance at

the newspaper, a quick bite to eat, and then it's off

to work. Basketball players travel so much that

they sometimes forget what town they're in. But

on the day of a game for a team on the road, the

routine rarely changes. Every morning, there's a

bus waiting outside the hotel to take them for their

morning workout.

Sam Forencich

JASON KIDD

The morning workout, also known as a

shootaround,

usually begins at 10:00. For the next hour or so, players will work up a light sweat, get a feel for the court and the baskets, and start thinking about the game ahead.

Garrett Ellwood

IN THE QUIET OF A NEAR-EMPTY ARENA, **EDDIE JONES** WORKS ON HIS LONG-RANGE JUMPER— SHOT, AFTER SHOT, AFTER SHOT.

Fernando Medina

PENNY HARDAWAY
STRETCHES OUT WITH HIS
ORLANDO TEAMMATES.

UNDER THE WATCHFUL EYE
OF COACH **DEL HARRIS**,
THE LOS ANGELES LAKERS
GO THROUGH A TOUGH
MORNING WORKOUT.

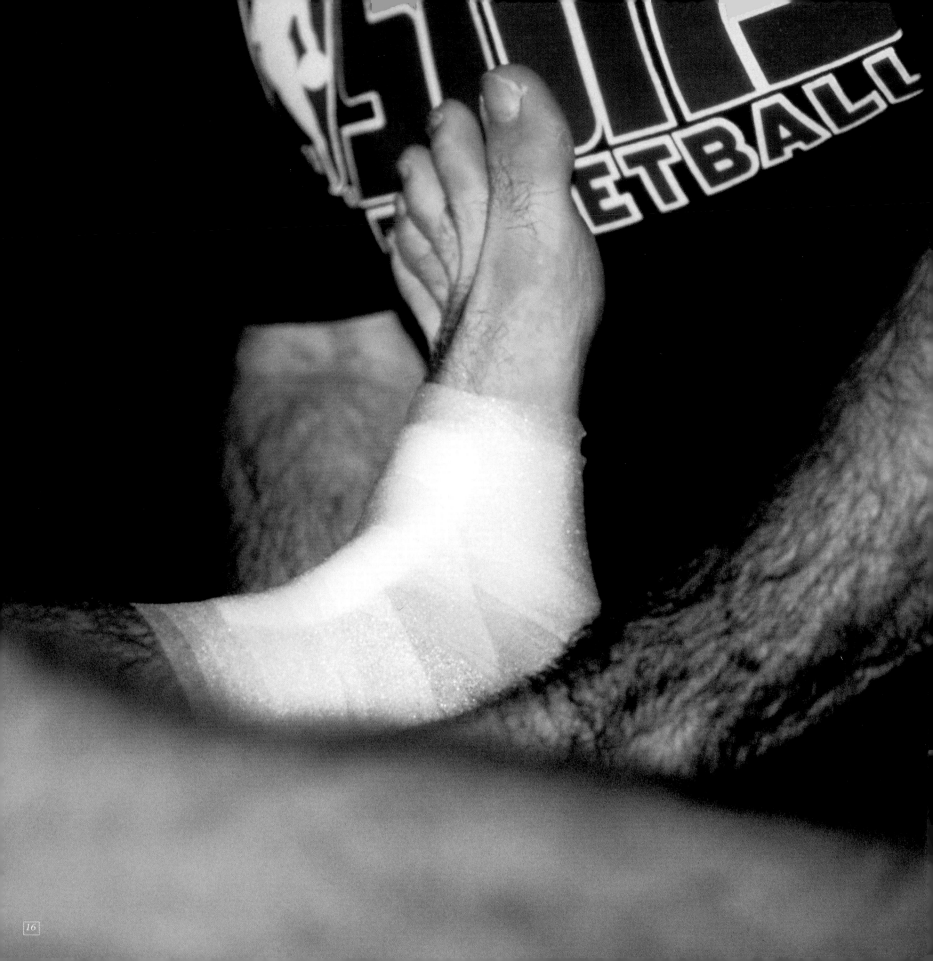

Sandy Tenuto

It's a long year: **82** games in the regular season alone.

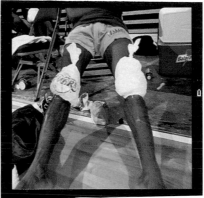

Andrew D. Bernstein

With that kind of grind, the body takes a beating. So it's vital

for players to take care of themselves. After the shootaround

they'll usually visit the trainer's room to get treatment for any

injuries. A few minutes in the whirlpool can do wonders.

(*From top to bottom*): **REX CHAPMAN**
SOAKS A TROUBLESOME LEFT ANKLE;
ICE BAGS SOOTH **EDDIE JONES'**
ACHING KNEES; **GLENN ROBINSON**
SITS DOWN TO A GOOD BOOK...
AND A NICE, WARM WHIRLPOOL.

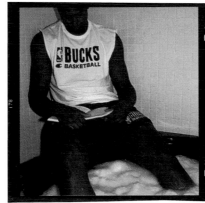

Gary Dineen

TOM GUGLIOTTA VISITS
WITH SCHOOL CHILDREN
IN SUPPORT OF THE NBA'S
"JUMPSTART TO READING"
PROGRAM.

STEPHON MARBURY

The afternoon of a night game is **personal time** for the players.
They may relax, make a public appearance, or donate time to a favorite charity.

KEVIN GARNETT

Some players may catch a movie, or go out for a meal with teammates, or take a quick nap back at the hotel.
If players are lucky enough to be home, they can take a few hours to spend time with their families.

NICK VAN EXEL

Mitchell Layton

WASHINGTON WIZARD **CHRIS WEBBER** TAKES A BREAK FROM THE HARDWOOD.

MITCH RICHMOND AND A YOUNG ADMIRER.

José Luis Villegas

Around 5:15,

the players return

to the arena. The

game is just over

two hours away

and there's lots

to do. Pretty soon

Michael Jordan

will exchange this

elegant designer

suit for the

uniform of the

Chicago Bulls.

MICHAEL JORDAN

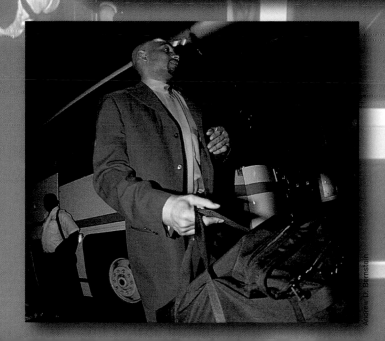

Andrew D. Bernstein

Gary Bassing

Andrew D. Bernstein

(From top to bottom):
**THEO RATLIFF,
ANFERNEE HARDAWAY,**
AND **GRANT HILL.**

CALIFORNIA CHARTER

3133

California CHARTER

Garrett Ellwood

Andrew D. Bernstein

There are many demands on the time of an

NBA player. He's not just an athlete; he's a

promoter. That's why the locker room is open

to the media from 6:00 until 6:45. Many

interviews are conducted during this time.

CEDRIC CEBALLOS SHARES
A LIGHT MOMENT DURING
A PRE-GAME TELEVISION
INTERVIEW. LATER ON, HE'LL BE
ALL BUSINESS.

DURING THE COURSE OF A SEASON PLAYERS ARE ASKED TO SIGN ALL KINDS OF THINGS: JERSEYS, PHOTOS, SCRAPS OF PAPER—EVEN SOCKS. HERE'S **MARCUS CAMBY** SIGNING A BASKETBALL FOR A GRATEFUL FAN.

Fans

who arrive early get a chance

to see their favorite players in

a more relaxed atmosphere.

Sometimes, there's even an

opportunity for an autograph.

HAKEEM OLAJUWON

Ray Amati

As game time approaches,

the busiest man

on the team is

the trainer.

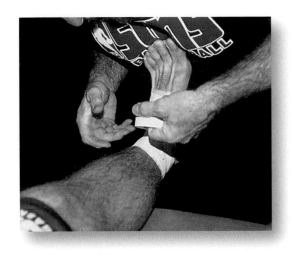 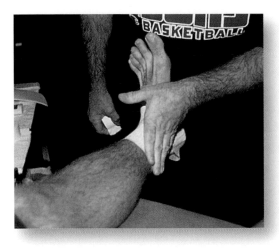 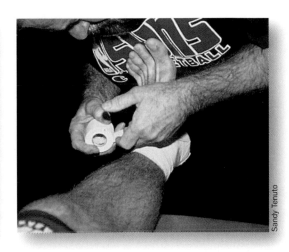

He checks injuries and wraps ankles.

He unravels a mile of athletic tape.

It's his job to make sure that each player is

physically prepared for the rigors of competition.

Without a trainer, the players' lives

would be a lot more difficult.

HEY, THAT TICKLES: A TRAINER
GOES TO WORK ON **LINDSEY HUNTER**
AS A TEAMMATE LOOKS ON.

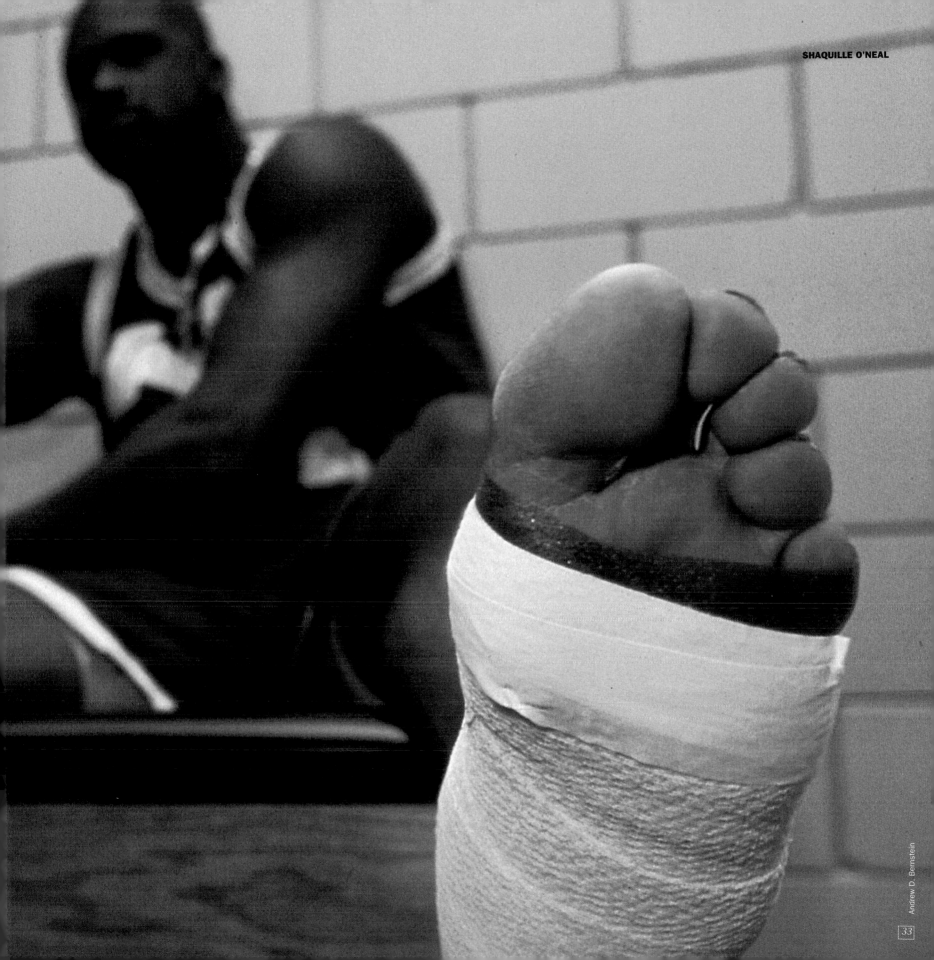

GEORGE KARL, HEAD COACH OF THE SEATTLE SUPERSONICS, REVIEWS THE GAME PLAN.

Each night brings a new opponent,

a new set of challenges

that must be addressed.

The pregame meeting begins

around 7:00.

STUDY TIME: **BILL BERTKA**, AN ASSISTANT
COACH FOR THE LAKERS, DIAGRAMS SOME
PLAYS. ONCE HIS TEAM UNDERSTANDS WHAT TO
EXPECT FROM AN OPPONENT, THEY'LL BE MUCH
BETTER PREPARED TO WIN THE GAME.

As tipoff draws near,

each player finds a way to

get ready

for the game.

Preparation is a matter of individual taste.

Some players sit quietly.

Some like to talk or joke around.

FORMER TEAMMATES AT
GEORGETOWN UNIVERSITY,
OTHELLA HARRINGTON AND
ALLEN IVERSON, CATCH UP
ON OLD TIMES.

THE SOLITUDE OF A SET OF HEADPHONES HELPS **MARCUS CAMBY** TUNE OUT THE PRESSURES BEFORE THE GAME.

Meanwhile, outside, the excitement builds.

Fans line up to purchase tickets and enter the arena.

The sense of **anticipation** is thick in the air.

Fans filter in, find their seats, and pick up refreshments.

A mascot might entertain the early arrivals.

Music fills the arena, putting everyone in the mood

for a great night of basketball.

41

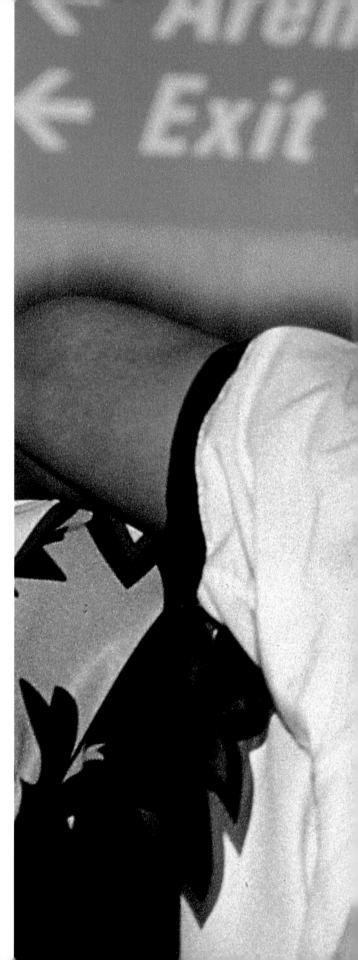

Basketball is a **team** game. Everyone strives toward a common goal. Moments before taking the floor for pregame warm-ups, the players huddle together in a corridor and remind each other that they are more than a collection of individuals. They are a team. If they want to win, they must play **together.**

Fernando Medina

PATRICK EWING AND **LARRY JOHNSON**

Christobal Perez

TONI KUKOC

At 7:20 both teams begin the familiar ritual
of warming up. To get ready for the game
they jog through layups, practice their
dribbling and shooting, and try to work up
a good sweat. Many players like to do a lot of

stretching

before the game because it helps them
avoid injuries.

THE BACK ACHES MORE NOW. THE
LONG ROAD JUST GETS LONGER. AT
AGE 34, **CHARLES BARKLEY** KNOWS
HE ISN'T A KID ANYMORE. BUT ONCE
THE GAME STARTS, HE'S READY TO
DEFEND HIS STATUS AS ONE OF THE
NBA'S 50 GREATEST PLAYERS EVER.

Chris Covatta

45

THE NUMBER ONE PICK IN THE 1995 NBA DRAFT, **JOE SMITH** SCORES POINTS, TEARS DOWN REBOUNDS, AND BLOCKS SHOTS. PLUS, HE'S PRETTY GOOD WITH A STICK OF BUBBLE GUM.

Jeff Feinking

AS GAME TIME DRAWS NEAR, A TEAM
TRAINER HELPS **SHAWN KEMP**
STRETCH (*REALLY S-T-R-E-T-C-H*)
HIS HAMSTRINGS.

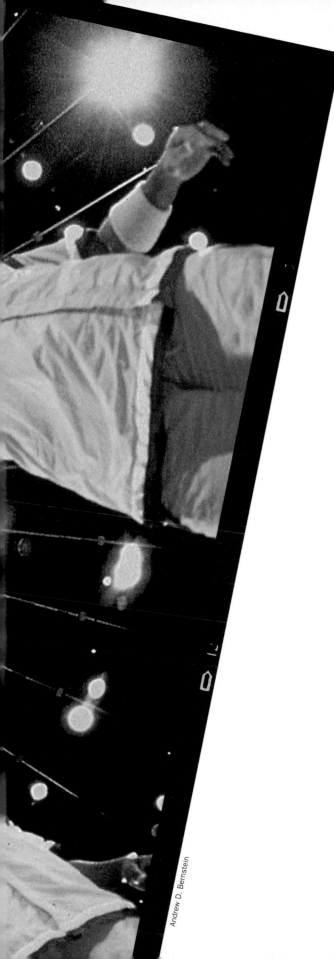

A few minutes before tipoff,

the captains

of both teams meet at

center court.

They receive instructions and explanations from

the officials. If there are any questions about the rules

governing the game, now is the time to ask.

When the meeting is over, the captains shake hands,

wish each other luck, and return to

their respective teams.

NBA Photo Library

Players gather in a circle around the bench.

The houselights dim.

The music stops.

It's time to introduce

the starting five

for each team.

Andrew D. Bernstein

Showtime.

Warm-ups are peeled off.

There's a final huddle

with the coach.

Teammates offer words

of encouragement.

Then the starters

take the floor.

Two of the tallest meet

at center court.

An official tosses

the ball high.

MUGGSY BOGUES
GETS INTENSE.

Tim O'Dell

The game is on.

Dave Sherman

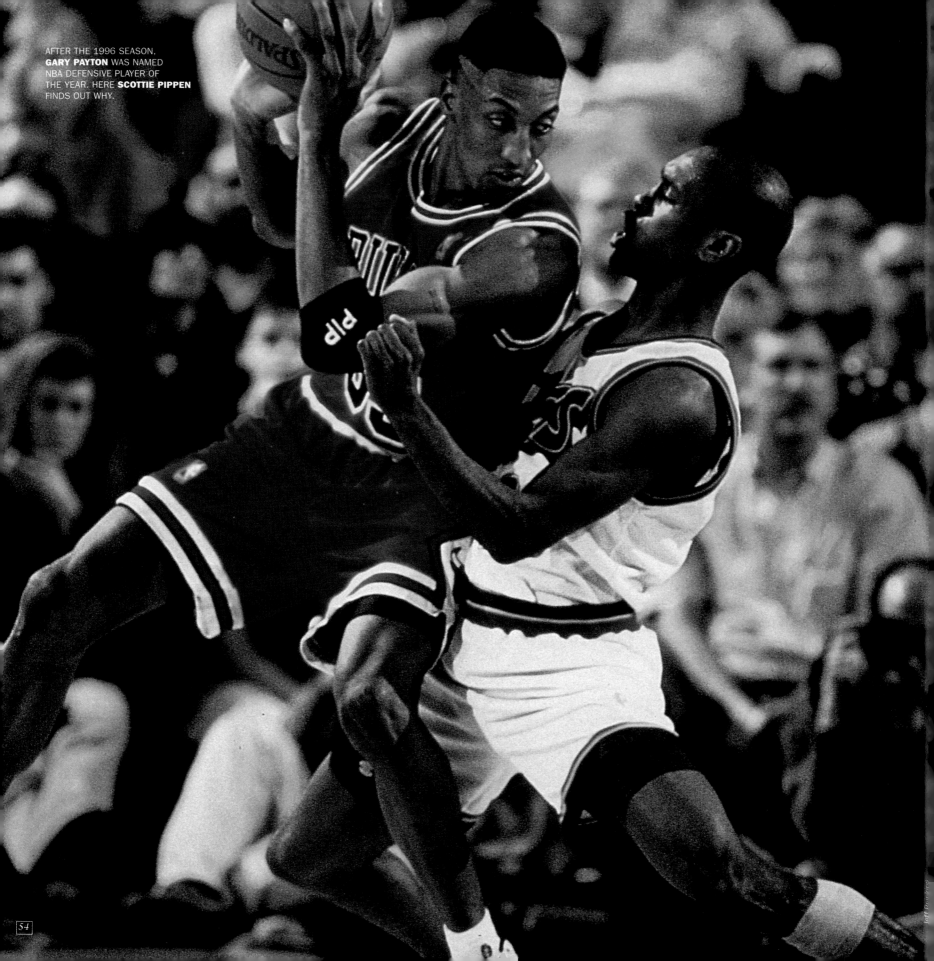

AFTER THE 1996 SEASON,
GARY PAYTON WAS NAMED
NBA DEFENSIVE PLAYER OF
THE YEAR. HERE **SCOTTIE PIPPEN**
FINDS OUT WHY.

54

Nathaniel S. Butler

ONE OF THE MOST ELECTRIFYING
PLAYERS IN THE NBA, ROOKIE
SENSATION **ALLEN IVERSON** LETS
FLY A BEHIND-THE-BACK PASS.

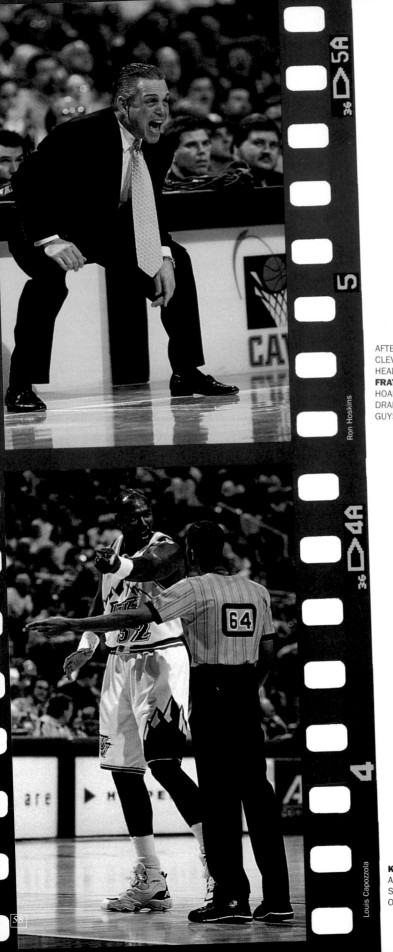

Ron Hoskins

AFTER A GAME,
CLEVELAND CAVALIERS
HEAD COACH **MIKE
FRATELLO** IS OFTEN
HOARSE AND PHYSICALLY
DRAINED. IMAGINE THE
GUYS WHO PLAYED!

Louis Capozzola

KARL MALONE
AND A REFEREE
SHARE A DIFFERENCE
OF OPINION.

PENNY HARDAWAY GOES BASELINE.

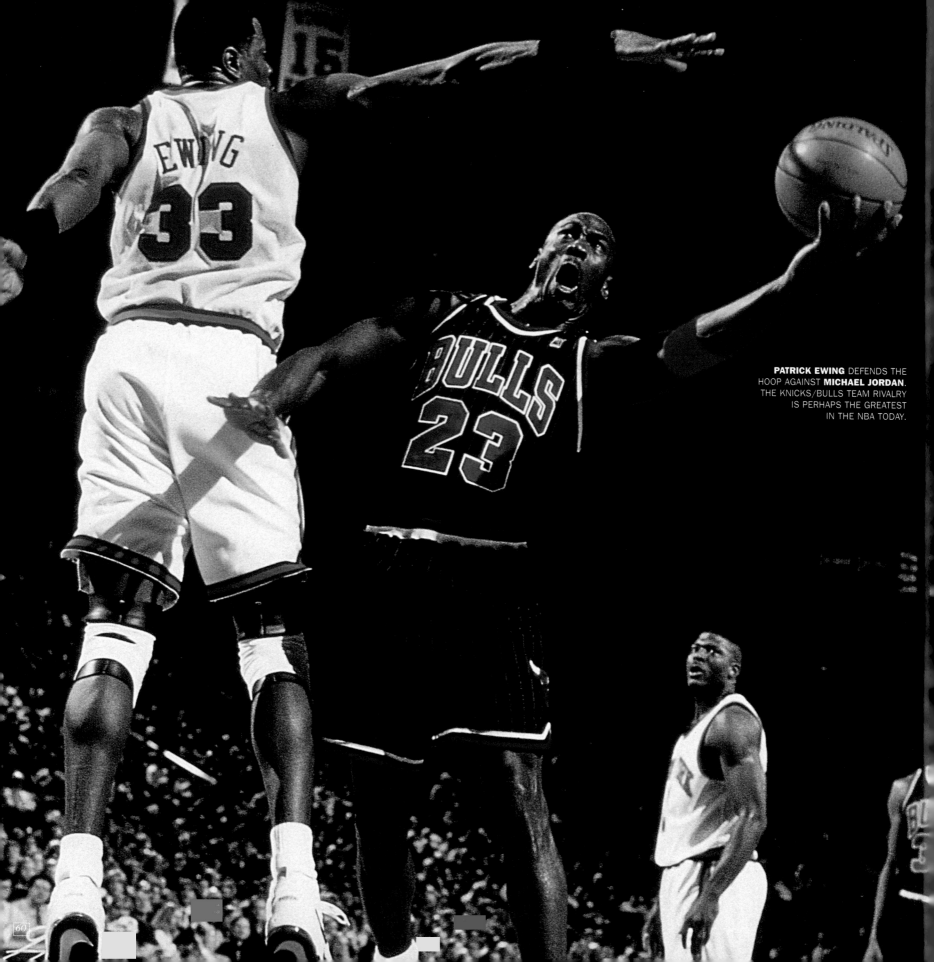

PATRICK EWING DEFENDS THE HOOP AGAINST **MICHAEL JORDAN**. THE KNICKS/BULLS TEAM RIVALRY IS PERHAPS THE GREATEST IN THE NBA TODAY.

(Clockwise, from top left) **ALONZO MOURNING** GOES UP AGAINST **DIKEMBE MUTOMBO**
AND **CHRISTIAN LAETTNER**; **GRANT HILL** GETS ACROBATIC; **HAKEEM OLAJUWON**
SHOWS HIS REVERSE JAM; **STEPHON MARBURY** TAKES TO THE AIR.

Exhausted from another night of work, the players return to the locker room.

Andrew D. Bernstein

It's a busy place.

Andrew D. Bernstein

The equipment manager scoops up dirty laundry.
The trainer cuts tape and applies ice to tender, swollen joints.

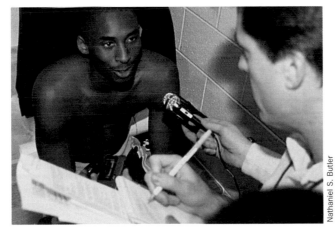

Nathaniel S. Butler

(*Top to bottom*) **EDDIE JONES**;
A TRAINER MAKES SMALL REPAIRS;
KOBE BRYANT GIVES A
POST-GAME INTERVIEW.

Reporters mill around, seeking quotes from key players.

The arena falls dark.

Players climb aboard a bus that will

take them back to the hotel or, perhaps,

the nearest airport. Then they're gone

again, into the night, flying to

another city...another game.